The Mind-Body Connection: Understanding the Link Between Mental and Physical Health

Dr. Micheal Lyon

Table of content

Chapter 1: The Science of the Mind-Body Connection

What is the mind-body connection?
The mind-body connection refers to the link between an individual's physical and mental states, and how they can affect one another. The mind-body connection is based on the idea that the mind and body are not separate entities, but rather they are interconnected and influence each other. For example, stress and other negative emotions can affect the body's physical health, while physical health can impact a person's mental and emotional well-being.

There is a growing body of research on the mind-body connection, which has shown that our thoughts, emotions, and behaviors can have a powerful impact on our physical health. Some of how the mind-body connection has been studied include the effects of stress on the immune system, the relationship between negative emotions and chronic diseases, and the role of behaviors such as exercise, nutrition, and sleep in promoting physical and mental health.

Understanding the mind-body connection can help promote overall health and well-being, as it allows individuals to take a holistic approach to their health and consider how their mental and emotional states may be impacting their physical health, and vice versa.

The mind-body connection is not just a theoretical concept, but rather it has been demonstrated through scientific research. For example, studies have shown that people who are under chronic stress or who have negative emotions such as anger or depression are more prone to certain health problems, including heart disease, high blood pressure, and weakened immune systems.

Many different factors can influence the mind-body connection, including genetics, environmental factors, and lifestyle habits. By understanding these factors, individuals can take steps to optimize their mental and physical health.

Many people have experienced firsthand how their mental and emotional states can affect their physical health. For example, feeling anxious or stressed can lead to physical symptoms such as an increased heart rate, stomachache, or headache. Conversely, physical illness or discomfort can impact an individual's mood and emotional well-being.

Some variovarioususd strategies can be used to support a healthy mind-body connection, such as stress management techniques, regular physical activity, a healthy diet, and getting enough sleep.

Research suggests that certain practices, such as mindfulness meditation, can be particularly effective in promoting a healthy mind-body connection. These practices involve paying attention to the present moment and cultivating a sense of calm and clarity, which can have numerous physical and mental health benefits.

The latest research on the mind-body connection

The study of the mind-body connection is an active area of research, and there have been many recent developments in our understanding of how mental and physical health are interconnected. Here are a few examples of some of the latest research on the mind-body connection:

There is growing evidence that the gut microbiome, or the collection of bacteria and other microorganisms that live in the digestive tract, can influence various aspects of health, including mental health. For example, research has shown that the gut microbiome can affect the production of neurotransmitters such as serotonin, which play a role in mood regulation.

Studies have also shown that certain behavioral factors, such as social support, can affect physical health outcomes. For example, research has found that people who have strong social connections tend to have better physical health, including a lower risk of heart disease and a stronger immune system.

Mindfulness-based interventions, such as mindfulness meditation, are effective in reducing stress and improving mental health outcomes, such as reducing anxiety and depression. Some research has also suggested that mindfulness practices may have physical health benefits, such as lowering blood pressure and improving immune function.

There is increasing evidence that chronic stress can hurt physical health, including increasing the risk of developing certain chronic conditions such as heart disease, diabetes, and certain cancers. Research is ongoing to understand the mechanisms underlying this relationship and to develop effective strategies for managing stress and promoting physical and mental health.

Some studies have suggested that certain types of physical activity, such as yoga and tai chi, may have particular benefits for mental health and the mind-body connection. For example, research has shown that yoga can reduce stress and improve mood, and that tai chi can improve balance and reduce the risk of falls in older adults.

There is evidence that how we think about our health and illness can influence our physical and mental well-being. For example, research has found that people who have a positive outlook and a sense of control over their health tend to have better physical health outcomes.

There is growing evidence that the environments in which we live, work, and play can have a significant impact on our health and well-being. For example, research has shown that living in areas with high levels of air pollution or noise can have negative effects on physical and mental health, while access to green spaces and natural environments can have positive effects.

Some research has suggested that the use of social media and other digital technologies may have both positive and negative effects on mental and physical health. For example, studies have found that social media use can provide social support and improve mental health in some cases, but it can also contribute to stress, anxiety, and other negative mental health outcomes in others.

These are just a few examples of the latest research on the mind-body connection. There is still much to learn about this complex and multifaceted relationship, and ongoing research is helping to deepen our understanding and inform the development of effective interventions for promoting mental and physical health.

How the mind and body communicate
There are many ways in which the mind and body communicate and influence each other. Here are a few examples:

The nervous system is a complex network of cells, tissues, and organs that carries information back and forth between the brain and the rest of the body. The nervous system allows the body to respond to changes in the environment and helps to regulate various functions such as heart rate, blood pressure, and digestion.

The endocrine system is another important system that plays a role in the mind-body connection. The endocrine system consists of glands that produce hormones, which are chemical messengers that help to regulate various bodily functions. Hormones can affect mood, energy levels, and other aspects of mental and physical health.

The immune system is also involved in the mind-body connection. The immune system helps to protect the body against illness and disease, and research has shown that stress and other negative emotions can weaken the immune system. On the other hand, some studies have suggested that positive emotions and social support can boost the immune system and help to promote health.

The gut microbiome, or the collection of bacteria and other microorganisms that live in the digestive tract, has been found to play a role in the mind-body connection. Research has shown that the gut microbiome can influence the production of neurotransmitters such as serotonin, which play a role in mood regulation.

The respiratory system, which includes the lungs and the airways, plays a role in the mind-body connection. How we breathe can affect our emotional state and vice versa. For example, rapid, shallow breathing can be a sign of anxiety, while slow, deep breaths can help to calm the mind and promote relaxation.

The cardiovascular system, which includes the heart and blood vessels, is also involved in the mind-body connection. Stress and other negative emotions can increase heart rate and blood pressure, while relaxation and positive emotions can have the opposite effect.

The skin, the largest organ in the body, also plays a role in the mind-body connection. Stress and other negative emotions can lead to physical symptoms such as skin rashes or hives, while relaxation and positive emotions can promote healthy skin.

The musculoskeletal system, which includes the bones, muscles, and joints, is also involved in the mind-body connection. Research has shown that chronic stress can lead to muscle tension and pain, while relaxation techniques such as massage and yoga can help to reduce muscle tension and improve physical and mental well-being.

The digestive system, which includes the stomach and intestines, is also involved in the mind-body connection. Stress and other negative emotions can affect digestion and lead to physical symptoms such as stomachache, while relaxation and positive emotions can promote healthy digestion.

These are just a few examples of how the mind and body communicate and influence each other. The mind-body connection is a complex and multifaceted relationship, and ongoing research is helping to deepen our understanding of the various mechanisms involved.

Chapter 2: The Impact of Stress on the Mind and Body

The physical effects of stress

Stress is the body's natural response to situations that it perceives as threatening or challenging. When you feel stressed, your body goes into "fight or flight" mode, releasing hormones such as adrenaline and cortisol to help you respond to the perceived threat. This can have a range of physical effects on the body, including:

1. Increased heart rate and blood pressure: Stress can cause your heart to beat faster and your blood vessels to constrict, which can increase your blood pressure.

2. Tight muscles: Stress can cause your muscles to tense up, especially in your neck, shoulders, and back.

3. Headaches: Stress can trigger tension headaches or migraines.

4. Digestive problems: Stress can cause digestive problems such as nausea, diarrhea, or constipation.

5. Insomnia: Stress can interfere with your sleep, making it difficult to fall asleep or stay asleep.

6. Exhaustion: Chronic stress can leave you feeling exhausted and drained.

7. Weak immune system: Stress can weaken your immune system, making you more prone to illness.

It's important to manage stress healthily, as chronic stress can have serious negative effects on your physical and mental health. Some ways to manage stress include exercising, practicing relaxation techniques such as deep breathing or meditation, and getting enough sleep.

The mental and emotional effects of stress

In addition to the physical effects of stress, it can also have significant mental and emotional effects. Some common mental and emotional symptoms of stress include:

- Anxiety: Stress can cause feelings of worry, fear, or nervousness.

- Depression: Stress can lead to feelings of sadness, hopelessness, or a lack of interest in activities.

- Irritability: Stress can make you more prone to feeling angry, frustrated, or irritable.

- Difficulty concentrating: Stress can make it harder to focus, remember things, or make decisions.

- Memory problems: Stress can interfere with your ability to remember things or recall information.

- Lack of motivation: Stress can drain your energy and make you feel less motivated to do things.

- Changes in appetite: Stress can cause changes in your appetite, leading to weight gain or loss.

- Low sex drive: Stress can decrease your desire for sex or physical intimacy.

It's important to manage stress healthily, as chronic stress can have serious negative effects on your mental and emotional health. Some ways to manage stress include exercising, practicing relaxation techniques such as deep breathing or meditation, and getting enough sleep.

Chapter 3: The Role of Emotions in Physical Health

Emotions play a significant role in physical health. Negative emotions such as stress, anger, and anxiety can weaken the immune system and lead to physical health problems. On the other hand, positive emotions such as happiness and gratitude can improve the immune system and overall physical health.

The connection between emotions and physical health

There is a strong connection between emotions and physical health. Emotions can affect the body's immune system and the production of hormones, which can impact physical health. Negative emotions such as stress, anger, and anxiety can weaken the immune system and lead to physical health problems, while positive emotions such as happiness and gratitude can improve the immune system and overall physical health.

For example, stress activates the body's stress response, which can lead to physical symptoms such as high blood pressure, heart problems, and digestion issues. Chronic stress can weaken the immune system, making a person more susceptible to illness.

Anger can also have negative effects on physical health. Chronic anger can lead to high blood pressure, heart problems, and even stroke. It is important to find healthy ways to manage and express anger, such as through exercise or talking to a therapist.

Anxiety can also have physical health consequences. Chronic anxiety can lead to digestive problems, sleep problems, and a weakened immune system. It is important to seek help for anxiety through therapy, medication, or other treatment options.

On the other hand, positive emotions can have a positive impact on physical health. Happiness and gratitude, for example, can boost the immune system and improve overall physical health. Engaging in activities that bring joy and practicing gratitude can improve physical health and well-being.

Overall, it is important to manage emotions and find healthy ways to cope with negative emotions to maintain physical health.

How to manage negative emotions and promote positive ones
There are several strategies you can use to manage negative emotions and promote positive ones:

1. Practice mindfulness: Being mindful means paying attention to the present moment in a nonjudgmental way. This can help you manage negative emotions and increase positive ones

by helping you to become more aware of your thoughts and feelings.

2. Engage in relaxation techniques: Relaxation techniques such as deep breathing, meditation, and yoga can help reduce stress and negative emotions.

3. Exercise regularly: Exercise has been shown to reduce stress and improve mood. Aim for at least 30 minutes of moderate-intensity activity, such as brisk walking, most days of the week.

4. Get enough sleep: Lack of sleep can lead to negative emotions such as irritability and anxiety. Aim for 7-9 hours of sleep per night.

5. Practice gratitude: Focusing on the things you are grateful for can improve your mood and increase positive emotions. Try keeping a

gratitude journal or sharing what you are grateful for with others.

6. Connect with others: Social support is important for managing negative emotions and promoting positive ones. Spend time with friends and family, and seek support when you need it.

7. Seek professional help: If you are struggling to manage negative emotions, consider seeking help from a mental health professional. A therapist can help you develop coping strategies and work through any underlying issues.

Chapter 4: Promoting Mind-Body Wellness

Simple techniques for maintaining a healthy mind-body connection

Many simple techniques can help maintain a healthy mind-body connection. Here are a few:

1. Exercise regularly: Physical activity has been shown to improve mental health and well-being.

2. Eat a healthy diet: A balanced diet that is rich in fruits, vegetables, and whole grains can help support both physical and mental health.

3. Get enough sleep: Adequate sleep is important for both physical and mental health.

4. Practice mindfulness: Mindfulness involves paying attention to the

present moment, without judgment. It can help reduce stress and improve overall well-being.

5. Take breaks from screens: Spending too much time on screens can be mentally draining. Taking breaks and engaging in other activities can help balance out screen time.

6. Seek social support: Connecting with others and building a support network can help improve mental health and overall well-being.

7. Practice self-care: Taking care of your own needs, such as through activities like meditation or self-care routines, can help improve mental health and well-being.

The benefits of mindfulness and meditation

Mindfulness is a mental state achieved by focusing one's awareness on the present moment, while calmly acknowledging and accepting one's feelings, thoughts, and bodily sensations, used as a therapeutic technique. Meditation is a practice in which an individual trains the mind or induces a mode of consciousness to realize some benefit.

There are numerous benefits to mindfulness and meditation, including:

- Reducing stress: Both mindfulness and meditation have been shown to help reduce stress and improve coping mechanisms for dealing with stress.

- Improving focus and concentration: These practices can help improve attention and focus, leading to improved productivity and overall well-being.

- Reducing anxiety: Both mindfulness and meditation can help reduce anxiety and improve symptoms of anxiety disorders.

- Improving sleep: These practices have been shown to improve sleep quality and can be helpful for individuals experiencing insomnia.

- Promoting emotional well-being: Mindfulness and meditation can help improve emotional well-being by promoting positive emotions and increasing self-awareness.

- Reducing chronic pain: These practices are effective in reducing chronic pain and improving pain management.

- Improving cardiovascular health: Both mindfulness and meditation have been linked to improved cardiovascular health, including lower blood pressure and improved heart rate variability.

How to create a healthy and balanced lifestyle

Creating a healthy and balanced lifestyle involves making choices that promote physical, mental, and emotional well-being. Here are some tips to help you create a healthy and balanced lifestyle:

- Make time for self-care: Take care of your own needs, such as through activities like exercise, good nutrition, and getting enough sleep.

- Set goals: Identify your goals and work towards them in a way that is realistic and sustainable.

- Find ways to manage stress: Find healthy ways to manage stress, such as through exercise, meditation, or talking to a friend or loved one.

- Engage in activities that bring joy: Find activities that bring you joy and make time for them in your life.

- Stay active: Incorporate physical activity into your daily routine. This can include activities like going for a walk, taking a yoga class, or playing a sport.

- Eat a healthy diet: Focus on eating a balanced diet that is rich in fruits, vegetables, and whole grains.

- Connect with others: Maintain strong relationships with friends and loved ones, and seek social support when needed.

- Find work-life balance: Maintain a healthy balance between work and other aspects of your life.

- Get enough sleep: Aim for 7-9 hours of sleep per night to ensure that you are well-rested and able to function at your best.

Conclusion

In conclusion, the mind-body connection is a powerful and complex relationship that plays a significant role in overall health and well-being. By understanding and embracing this connection, we can take steps to improve both our mental and physical health. Whether through practices like mindfulness and meditation, making healthy lifestyle choices, or seeking support from others, there are many ways to nurture and support the mind-body connection. By doing so, we can improve our quality of life and pave the way for a happier, healthier future.